PREDATOR VS PREY

Dolphin Vs Fish

Mary Meinking

Raintree

www.raintreepublishers.co.uk
Visit our website to find out
more information about
Raintree books.

To order:

☎ Phone 0845 6044371

🖷 Fax +44 (0) 1865 312263

✉ Email myorders@raintreepublishers.co.uk

Customers from outside the UK please telephone +44 1865 312262

Raintree is an imprint of Capstone Global Library Limited,
a company incorporated in England and Wales having its
registered office at 7 Pilgrim Street, London, EC4V 6LB –
Registered company number: 6695582

Edited by Rebecca Rissman, Dan Nunn,
    and Catherine Veitch
Designed by Joanna Hinton Malivoire
Levelling by Jeanne Clidas
Picture research by Hannah Taylor
Production by Victoria Fitzgerald
Originated by Capstone Global Library
Printed and bound in China by CTPS

ISBN 978 1 40621 870 1
14 13 12 11 10
10 9 8 7 6 5 4 3 2 1

British Library Cataloguing in Publication Data
Meinking, Mary.
Dolphin vs fish. -- (Predator vs prey)
591.5'3-dc22
A full catalogue record for this book is available from the
British Library.

Acknowledgements
We would like to thank the following for permission
to reproduce photographs: Alamy Images p. 29 (©
WaterFrame); ardea.com pp. 4 (© Ken Lucas), 7 (© Ken
Lucas); Corbis pp. 8 (Specialist Stock), 13 (Ralph A.
Clevenger), 28 (Specialist Stock); Getty Images pp. 14
(Barcroft Media/ Eric Cheng), 15 (Alexander Safonov), 20
(Barcroft Media/ Jason Heller), 21 (Alexander Safonov), 23
(Alexander Safonov), 25 (National Geographic/ Paul Nicklen),
6 (Gallo Images/ Rod Haestler); naturepl.com pp. 12 (Mark
Carwardine), 18 (Doug Perrine), 19 (Doug Perrine); NHPA p.
27 (Franco Banfi); Photolibrary pp. 5 (age footstock), 9 (age
fotostock/ Michael S Nolan), 10 (Oxford Scientific/ Doug
Allan), 11 (WaterFrame/ Franco Banfi), 16 (WaterFrame/
Franco Banfi), 17 (Peter Arnold Images), 22 (Peter Arnold
Images/ Doug Perrine), 24 (Peter Arnold Images/ Doug
Perrine), 26 (WaterFrame/ Franco Banfi).

Cover photographs of a common dolphin reproduced with
permission of Corbis (Specialist Stock), and a Pacific sardine
reproduced with permission of ardea.com (Ken Lucas).

We would like to thank Michael Bright for his invaluable help
in the preparation of this book.

Every effort has been made to contact copyright holders of
material reproduced in this book. Any omissions will
be rectified in subsequent printings if notice is given to the
publisher.

Some words are shown in bold, **like this**. You can find
out what they mean by looking in the glossary.

Contents

Fin to fin combat

Teeth pierce! Tails splash! Two animals battle in the sea. Here's the cleverest animal in the sea, the dolphin. It's pitted against a shiny challenger, the sardine. This cool water fish is set for the clash to begin.

sardine

dolphin

DID YOU KNOW?
A dolpin will help an
injured person in the sea.

The competitors live in the ocean. Both have strengths that will help them in this battle.

PREDATOR
common dolphin

LENGTH: 260 centimetres

WEIGHT: 135 kilograms

SWIMMING SPEED: 40 kilometres an hour

Key

 where common dolphins and Pacific sardines live

PREY
Pacific sardine

LENGTH: 18 centimetres

WEIGHT: 0.15 kilograms

SWIMMING SPEED: 8 kilometres an hour

Sharp hunter

Dolphins have 200 pointed teeth! They do not chew their food. Their sharp teeth hold the slippery fish. Then they swallow them whole!

teeth

blowhole

DID YOU KNOW?

Dolphins are **mammals.** They need to come up to breathe every 8 to 10 minutes. A dolphin breathes through a **blowhole** on the top of its head.

School's out!

Sardines live in groups called schools or **shoals.** There can be millions of sardines in each shoal. Sometimes large shoals are 15 kilometres long!

shoal

DID YOU KNOW?

Sardine shoals swim like they are one fish. When a few sardines change direction, the whole shoal turns.

Who's hungry?

Dolphins are **carnivores**, or meat eaters. They eat octopus, shrimp, eel, and small fish. To grow healthy dolphins need fat in their diet. So they like to eat oily sardines.

DID YOU KNOW?
Sardines eat tiny living things called **plankton.** Plankton are smaller than the full stop at the end of this sentence.

Greatest shoal on Earth

Millions of sardines swim together in giant **shoals**. They are called sardine runs. **Pods**, or groups, of common dolphins follow the sardine runs. But how can they catch fish from the wide stream of sardines swimming by?

sardine run

pod

The dolphins dive into the sardine **shoal**. They swim at the sardines to **herd** thousands of them away from the main shoal. The sardines are afraid. They group together in a ball. They are safer in a ball.

It is more difficult for a dolphin to pick out one sardine from a big group of twisting, flashing fish.

The sardine ball is the size of a tennis court. The ball is called a **baitball**. The dolphins push the baitball up towards the **surface**. The sardines are trying to escape. The dolphins have surrounded them.

baitball

18

The dolphins swim around the **baitball**. They pack the sardines closer together. Some of the dolphins are like cowboys, keeping the sardines **herded** together. Others dive into the ball to eat. The dolphins take turns, making sure they all get something to eat!

Sharks come in from below to eat some sardines.

22

Birds called gannets dive down from the sky in to the **baitball**. The water is wild with activity!

gannet

After 20 minutes it's all over. A few lucky sardines remain. They escape and continue with the others in the sardine run. The **baitball** that was lost to the **predators** was just a small part of the giant **shoal**.

And the winner is...

...the dolphin! These team players worked together to catch their fill of sardines.

DID YOU KNOW?
Dolphins need to eat 9 kilograms of fish every day. That's like eating 300 fish fingers every day!

What are the odds?

When the dolphin **herds** sardines in **baitballs**, even if it misses one fish there will be hundreds more swimming by. The dolphin is cleverer than the fish. Its large brain helps it solve problems. It's mastered how to catch lots of sardines.

DID YOU KNOW?
Dolphins **communicate** with each other by whistling and making click sounds.

Glossary

baitball sardines that dolphins steer into a ball for food

blowhole opening on the top of an animal's head through which it breathes air

carnivore animal that eats meat

communicate give information to others

herd control or steer a group of animals

mammal warm-blooded animal that feeds its young milk

plankton tiny living things that float in the water

pod group of dolphins

predator animal that hunts other animals

prey animal that is hunted by other animals for food

shoal large group of fish swimming together

surface top part of something

Find out more

Books

Face to Face with Dolphins,
Flip and Linda Nicklin (National Geographic
Children's Books, 2007)

Watching Dolphins in the Oceans,
Elizabeth Miles (Heinemann Library, 2007)

Whales and Dolphins, Susanna Davidson
(Usborne, 2008)

Websites

**http://kids.nationalgeographic.com/kids/
animals/creaturefeature/bottlenose-dolphin**
This website gives facts about dolphins, such
as where they live, and compares their size
to humans.

http://www.dolphinkind.com/
Visit this website to learn fun facts about
dolphins, how to make sounds like dolphins, and
how to help dolphins.

Index